WRITING AND
COOPERATIVE LEARNING

Social Skills ● Pre-writing Activities
Publishing Ideas ● Group Writing Projects

Written by: Marzella Brown

Illustrated by: Doreen Rivera, Blanqui Apodaca, Keith Vasconcelles, Theresa Wright

Teacher Created Materials, Inc.
P. O. Box 1214
Huntington Beach, CA 92647
©1990 Teacher Created Materials, Inc.
Made in U. S. A.
ISBN 1-55734-110-9

TABLE OF CONTENTS

INTRODUCTION

Writing and Cooperative Learning is the fourth book in Teacher Created Materials' cooperative learning series for students in grades 2-5. This 48 page book provides directions and patterns for 20 group projects which engage students in the writing process.

Writing and cooperative learning are natural partners! Brainstorming for ideas, shared editing and proofreading, cooperative "publishing," and other group activities are all part of the skill building activities in this book. Students involved in these projects will have a positive experience with writing that puts an emphasis on group, rather than individual, products.

Each writing project (mysteries, factual, descriptive, tall tales, research, and more) is prefaced by a list of needed materials and a pre-writing activity. The pre-writing activity is designed to stimulate thinking and provide a reservoir of ideas that can be used when writing begins. Brainstorming, literature models, and art prompts are some of the techniques used to get the creative process started.

Writing and Cooperative Learning also includes many patterns, instructions, and helpful illustrations for producing final written products in interesting forms. Fold-out books, books with moveable parts, patterns for book covers, shapes for writing on, unusual ways to display and share written work are among the many ideas for "publishing" student's writing.

Teachers will find in *Writing and Cooperative Learning* a wonderful collection of ideas that will encourage writing in a group setting. The projects produced make delightful displays so that writing can be shared, appreciated, and celebrated.

NOTE TO THE TEACHER

Editing each other's work is one of the repeated activities in *Writing and Cooperative Learning.* Students need to understand the purpose of editing so they can help each other in a constructive manner. They should know that all good writers have their work edited because it is often difficult to catch one's own errors. Therefore, the teacher should conduct lessons that will show children how to give constructive criticism without destroying ideas. The author should understand how to accept the editor's suggestions without feeling offended. A spirit of supportive cooperation should prevail.

MYSTERY BOX

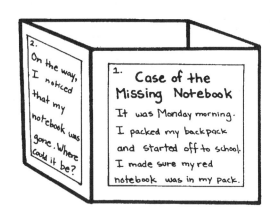

Materials:

- **A square box for each group**

- **4 index cards (or paper cut to fit sides of boxes) for each group**

- **Glue**

Pre-writing Activity:

Ask students if they have read or seen a mystery, or played a mystery game. You might like to read from an *Encyclopedia Brown* book by Donald J. Sobol. During the discussion elicit the idea that clues lead to the solution of a mystery.

Writing Project:

1. Divide the class into small groups. Tell each group to choose a mystery story starter such as the following:

   The Case of the Missing Notebook
   The Case of the Disappearing Lunches
   The Mixed Up Homework
   The Bent Key
   The Lost Diamond Ring

2. Each group should number their cards from 1 to 4. Students should work together to write a short mystery story making sure it includes clues but leaving off the solution. Editing tasks may be divided among group members. One person could check for grammar errors; another, spelling; the third, fluency; and the last person could make sure the story includes appropriate clues. The story should be divided into four sections and written, in order, on the cards. Then the cards should be glued onto the sides of the box.

3. Groups exchange boxes. Members can take turns reading the mystery. Then each group member should write a possible solution and place it in the box.

4. Return the box to its original group so they can read the solutions.

SOUND BOOKS

Materials:

- **Paper for book covers and pages**
- **Crayons**

Pre-writing Activity:

Have students think about how authors convey sounds to their readers. If we want someone to think of a particular sound when we are writing, we must use words that describe the sound. List sound words on the board including words that actually are the sound like, "har har" or "ker-choo."

Writing Project:

Have students work in small groups to write a story that includes lots of sounds. It could include sounds that are unusual, scary, loud, animal, quiet, city, night, etc. The group should make a list of the sound words they want to include in their book after choosing a topic. Then they should work together to write and illustrate their book. Remind them not to forget to edit their work before assembling the sound book. When students read their books to each other, they can make the sounds they have written about.

WHAT'S BEHIND THE DOOR?

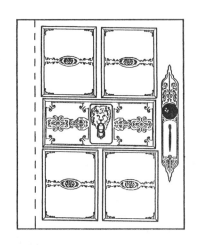

> *Materials:*
>
> - **Copy of door pattern (page 7) for each group**
> - **Writing paper**
> - **Crayons**

Pre-writing Activity:

Children are always curious about the unknown and look forward to a surprise. Draw a large door on the chalkboard. In its center put a question mark. Ask students what they think is behind the door. List their suggestions.

Writing Project:

Divide the students into small groups. Give each group one door pattern (page 7) and each student writing paper. Have each group choose something to be behind their door. Then each group member should title their paper, "What's Behind the Door?" They should write a riddle, paragraph, or rhyme giving hints. As a group they should select one person to illustrate what's behind the door after discussing what the drawing should include. Someone should color and cut out the door pattern. And, before displaying their work, students should work together to edit and proofread each other's writing. The left edge of the door pattern should be folded back at the dashed line and glued so that it covers the illustration and can be opened to reveal what's behind the door.

Mount the papers in a long row. Following the last piece of writing, mount the door with its hidden picture. Students may want to add captions under each writing paper directing readers to "Read the next selection;" "You're getting warm;" etc.

DOOR PATTERN

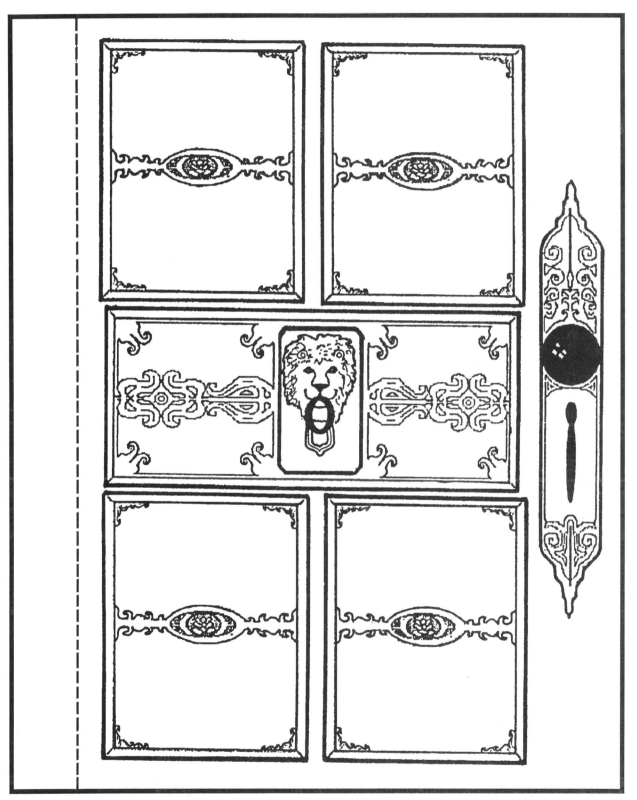

Fold back on dashed line. Paste the folded edge to paper so that the door can open and close.

DIAL-A-MEAL

Materials:

- **One copy of pages 9 and 10 for each group reproduced or glued onto heavy paper**
- **Writing paper**
- **Crayons**
- **Metal paper fasteners**

DIAL - A - MEAL

BOOK

Pre-writing Activity:

Put this heading on the chalkboard: "Favorite Meals." Ask several students to name their favorite meal eaten at home. List them and ask the students to tell everything included in the meal and how it is prepared.

Writing Project:

Divide the class into small groups. Tell them that they are going to write about their favorite meal, then put their meals together to make a dial-a-meal book. Each member should do the following:

1. Think of the favorite meal they enjoy eating at home.

2. Write what foods are included in the meal.

3. Tell how each food is prepared.

4. Think of a fancy name for the meal and write it at the top of the paper. For example, Old Fashioned Hot Dog on a Bun, Meatball and Potato Special, or Turkey with All the Trimmings.

5. Illustrate the meal at the bottom of the paper.

6. Sign their name.

Each group should color and assemble the cover for the Dial-A-Meal book (directions and patterns on pages 9 and 10). Put all of the papers together and number the pages. Write the names and page number of each meal in the cut-out space on the hamburger. Staple the cover and pages together. Turn the dial to see what everyone's favorite meal is and find the page to read all about it!

DIRECTIONS FOR DIAL-A-MEAL BOOK COVER

Reproduce pages 9 and 10 on heavy paper. Cut out wheel (p. 9) and **space** in hamburger (p. 10). **DO NOT CUT OUT HAMBURGER.** Attach wheel to back of hamburger with paper fastener through center dots. You may want to use hole reinforcers for extra durability.

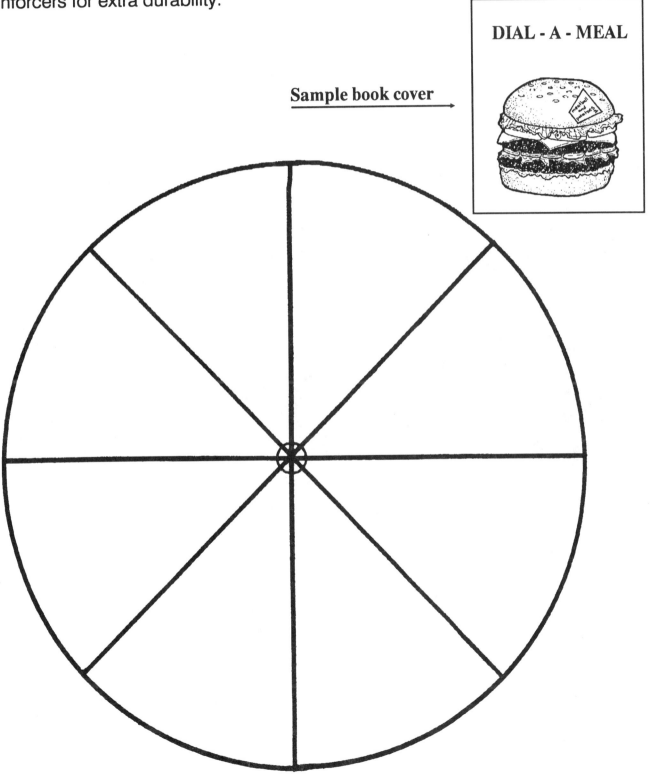

Sample book cover ⟶

DIAL - A - MEAL

DIAL-A-MEAL BOOK

Cut

Out

INSIDE MY HEAD

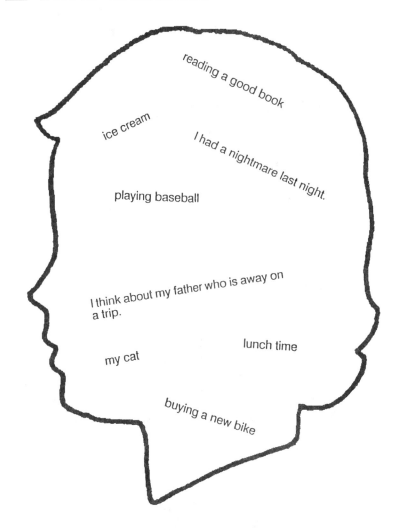

Materials:

- **White construction paper**
- **Projector or light**
- **Crayons**

Inside the silhouette:
reading a good book
ice cream
I had a nightmare last night.
playing baseball
I think about my father who is away on a trip.
lunch time
my cat
buying a new bike

Pre-writing Activity:

Talk with students about the many thoughts "inside their head." Even their dreams are thoughts that occur while they are asleep. Have some students share some of the things that are on their minds. Write these on the board.

Make an outline silhouette of each student's head by using a projector or light to shine on a piece of paper taped to the wall. Have each student stand sideways between the light source and the paper. Caution them not to look directly into the light. Move them until the shadow of their head fits onto the paper. Trace around the edge of the shadow with crayon.

Writing Project:

Inside their silhouette each student should write what they have been thinking about throughout the day, their dreams, wishes, or goals in life. They may write words, phrases, or whole sentences. After they have completed their writing, put students into small groups. Have them take turns sharing their information. When everyone has shared their thoughts, group members can ask each other questions. Example: Student's thought—"I think about traveling to faraway places." Question: "What places would you like to visit?" Stress taking turns and sharing ideas.

DISCOUNTS FOR KIDS

Materials:

- **Newspapers, magazines, and catalogs**
- **Paper, Glue**
- **Scissors, Crayons**

Pre-writing Activity:

Ask students how many of them like to find a good bargain. How many of them like to buy things when they are on sale? Make a list of some of the things students or their parents have bought when they were on sale. Ask them how they found out about the sale. Establish that ads on TV and radio or in newspapers and catalogs are good sources for news about sales.

Writing Project:

Divide the class into small groups. Each group should choose a shopping category; e.g., athletic shoes, sportswear, video games, toys, books, arts and crafts, etc. After selecting the category, they are to find items in that category that can be bought at a discount. Use newspapers, assign for homework, or let children create the item and its discount. Each member should write an advertisement for an item in the category. The name and address of the store in which the item can be purchased, when the sale begins and ends, and any other pertinent information should be included. The item should be pictured with a drawing or an illustration cut from newspapers, magazines, or catalogs.

Discounts for Kids

Toy rockets

Usually $10.95

Sale price $5.98

Have the greatest fun ever!

Get them at

TGM's Market

573 S. 9th St.

Sale Sat. to Tues., May 9 - 12

FANTASTIC FACTS

Materials:

- **Construction paper or tagboard to be used for book covers**

- **Writing paper**

Pre-writing Activity:

Discuss setting records with the children. Sports records will probably be a familiar area for discussion. Ask them if any of them have seen **The Guiness Book of World Records**. Show a copy and read some of the unusual records reported. Some of them seem "fantastic" or hard to believe.

Writing Project:

Divide the students into small groups. Tell them that they are going to write a book of fantastic facts about their classmates. Each child should choose a group member (make sure there are no duplicates) and think of something that person does, eats, or wears. Then exaggerate it to turn it into a fantastic fact. For example, if Janet is good at jumping rope, her "fact" might be, "Janet jumped rope and blew bubbles at the same time for 23 hours without stopping." Facts that may hurt someone's feelings are not acceptable. They should edit and proofread each other's writing and draw a picture to go with the fact. Collect all stories and make a class book of records.

Janet jumped rope and blew bubbles for 23 hours.

SURVIVAL TECHNIQUES

Materials:

- **Note size paper**
- **Large manila envelope for each group**

Pre-writing Activity:

Ask students what it would be like to live in the jungle (or on the moon, in a cave, on a mountaintop, etc.). What things do they need to have and know to survive in the chosen environment? Make a list of the suggestions on the board. Then tell them that they have a lot of school and family survival techniques that they may not even realize. Ask them what they need to know or have to survive in school, with younger or older brothers and sisters, doing homework, cleaning their room, etc.

Writing Project:

Divide the students into groups. Tell them to select, as a group, a "How to Survive..." title. It can be an exotic location or an everyday one. (Maybe they'd like to choose one of each kind.) On the front of the envelope write the chosen title. Students are to write their suggestions for survival on the notepaper and deposit them in the envelopes which can be hung around the room. When the project is completed, everyone can read the suggestions and learn more about survival techniques.

How To Survive As A Third Grader

How To Survive In A Jungle

How To Survive A Younger Brother

TREASURE CHEST

Materials:

- **Copy of treasure chest (page 16) for each student**

- **Crayons, Glue, Scissors**

- **Brown lunch bag for each group**

Pre-writing Activity:

Ask students if anyone has ever been on a treasure hunt. What were they looking for? What other kinds of things might be found on a treasure hunt? Talk about pirate treasure and modern day treasure hunts by divers looking for sunken ships. Make a list of "treasures" on the board. Elicit non-materialistic treasures (e.g.,love and health) and wishes that would be a treasure if they came true (e.g., a trip to Disney World). List these also.

Writing Activity:

Divide the class into small groups. Pass out a copy of the treasure chest to all of the group members. Have students follow these directions:

1. On the spaces above the dashed lines on the chest write a message about a treasure, something special, or a wish. Group members should help each other with the writing task.

2. Fold on dashed lines so that the message is hidden and the top meets the bottom of chest.

3. Glue the lock to the front of the chest, sealing it.

4. Color the chest and lock.

5. Decorate the lunch bag. Put all of the group's treasure chests inside the bag. Decide on a place to hide it in the classroom. Do not discuss this with the other groups in class.

6. Work together to write directions to the hidden treasure, then make a map. Someone in the group can draw the map and someone can write the directions. Hide the bag according to the map. (Teacher should allow one group to hide their bag at a time.)

7. Give your directions to the other groups in the class.

8. The group that finds the treasure gets to unlock the chests and read the messages.

TREASURE CHEST PATTERN

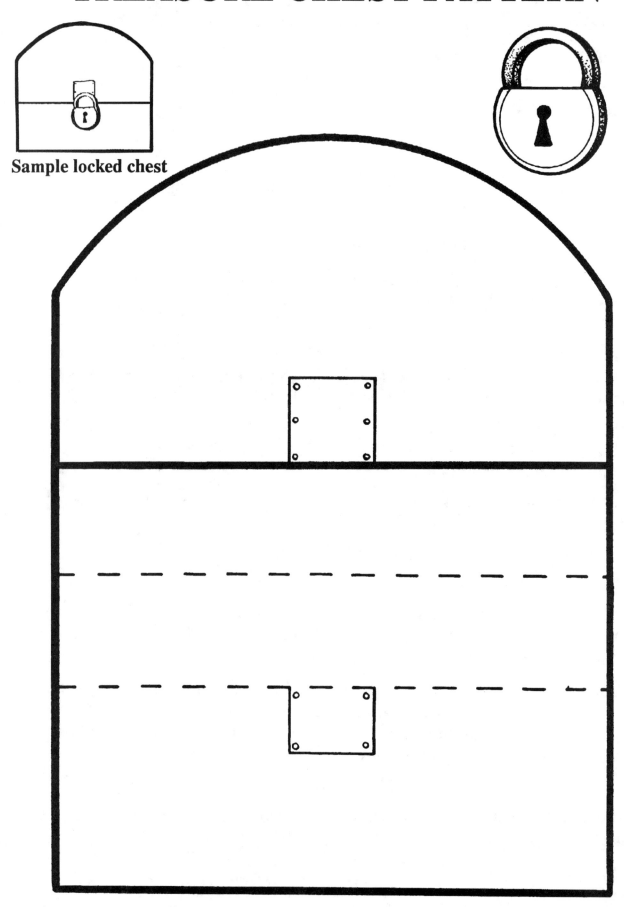

Sample locked chest

A BOOK OF LISTS

> **Materials:**
> - Paper
> - Crayons

Pre-writing Activity:

Talk to the students about how people often make lists to help them remember things; for example, a shopping list or a list of things to do. What are some lists that people in your family make? Lists can also be made of things in a certain category like types of automobiles or large cities. Select a category and make a list on the chalkboard of things in that category as a model for students.

Writing Project:

Divide the class into small groups. Each group should brainstorm for categories for lists they would like to make. Then they should work together to complete a list of things in each chosen category, researching if necessary. An illustration of one or more items on the list should be made on a separate piece of paper. When all groups have finished their lists and illustrations, they can be put together to make a class Book of Lists.

Some possible categories:

Cartoon Characters

Favorite TV Shows

Superheroes

Excuses for Not Doing Homework

Ball Games

Flavors of Ice Cream

Things to Do When You Are Bored

Sea Animals

Kinds of Natural Disasters

Native American Tribes

TALL TALES

Materials:

- **Continuous form computer paper (or attached sheets--top to bottom--of 8 1/2" x 11" paper)**

- **Tall tale characters from pages 19 to 26**

- **Scissors, Glue, Crayons**

Pre-writing Activity:

Read some tall tales to the class. Paul Bunyan and Pecos Bill are two possibilities. Point out that exaggeration is what makes a tale tall. Have students name some of the exaggerations in the stories just read. List them on the board.

Writing Project:

Divide the class into small groups. Members should decide which character from pages 19-26 they would like to write a tall tale about. They should brainstorm and choose a title for the story. Give each group 6 (or number determined by teacher) sections of computer paper. These tales are really tall, so the paper should be used lengthwise.

Divide these jobs among group members:

1.   Color the character.

2.   Cut out the face.

3.   Glue the character to the top sheet of the paper.

4.   Write the title above the character.

Work together to write the story. Make a rough draft and edit it together before copying it on to the paper under the character's head. The writing task may be divided so that each person writes one exaggerated feat of the character for each page of paper.

The group may want to work together to write a grand finale ending for the last sheet.

Here are some sample titles for the character pictures:

The Mysterious Old Man	Diving Denise
Fishy Tales	Jungle Jade or Archaeologist Ashai
Pirate Pedro	Spaceman Spenser
Round 'Em Up Jones	The Perfect Princess

TALL TALE CHARACTER

TALL TALE CHARACTER

TALL TALE CHARACTER

TALL TALE CHARACTER

TALL TALE CHARACTER

#110 Writing and Cooperative Learning

TALL TALE CHARACTER

24

TALL TALE CHARACTER

TALL TALE CHARACTER

TIME MACHINE

Materials:

- Copy of time machine and wheel (pages 28 and 29) on heavy paper for each group

- Paper for book pages cut to the shape of the time machine

- Scissors, Crayons

- Metal paper fasteners, Stapler

Pre-writing Activity:

Ask the students what it was like to live in the past. When they reply, ask them to date the time they are speaking of. Have them think about the clothing, transportation, recreation, etc. from that era. Put the date on the chalkboard and list ideas beneath it. Now have students think about a date in the future. What might life be like then? Record their ideas. As a class, choose a variety of dates to be written about. List them; for example, 5000 B.C., 500 A.D., 1492, 1776, 1940, 2001, 3050.

Writing Project:

Divide the students into groups. Have them assemble a cover for their book following these directions:

1. Color and cut out the Time Machine (page 28).

2. Cut out the opening on the machine.

3. Cut out the wheel (page 29).

4. Use a metal paper fastener through the X's to attach the wheel behind the time machine.

5. To make pages for the book, trace around the time machine and cut out.

Have students work in pairs within their groups to write stories for the time machine book using the chosen dates. For dates in the future they can make up their stories and for dates in the past they should do research for authenticity. It might be fun for each pair to have both a future and a past date. After the stories are illustrated, edited and proofread by the group, they can be copied onto the specially-shaped paper and assembled into a book by stapling to the time machine cover along the left edge. (Be careful not to catch the wheel in the staples.)

In the opening on the time machine write the dates that the group has written about and the page number on which to find information about that date. Now the "Table of Contents" of this unique book can be read by turning the wheel of the time machine.

TIME MACHINE BOOK COVER

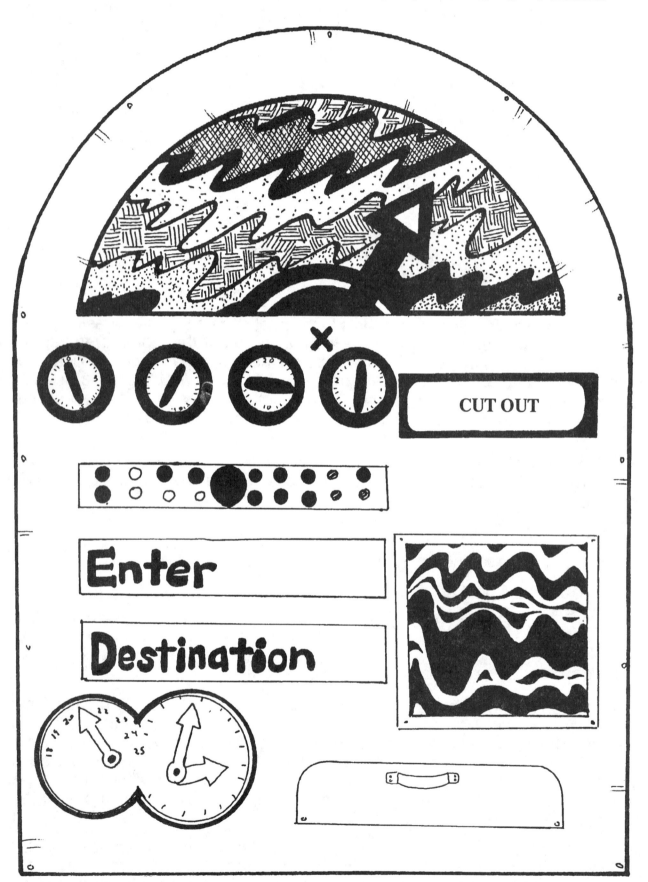

CUT OUT

Enter

Destination

TIME MACHINE BOOK COVER
(cont.)

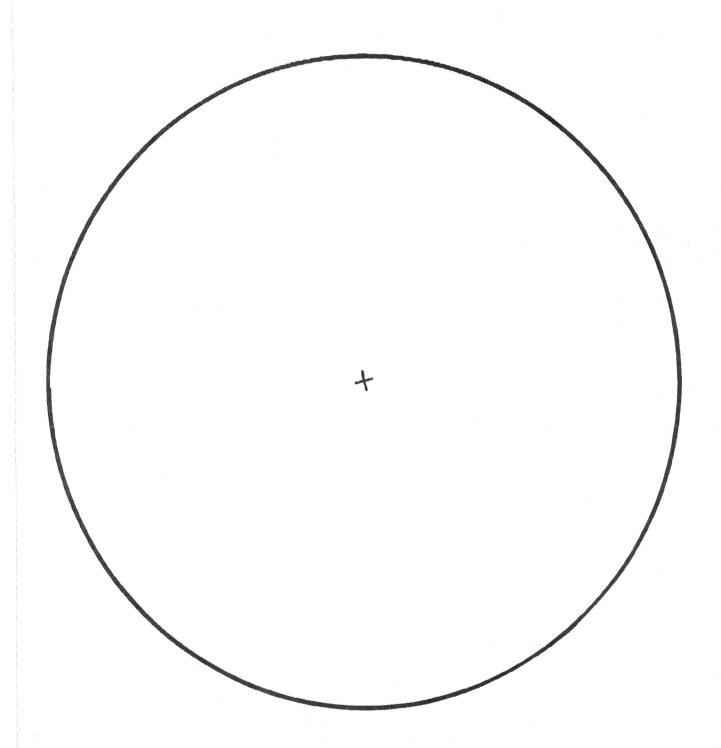

(cont.)

LET YOUR FEET DO THE TALKING

Materials:

- **Construction paper**
- **Scissors**

Pre-writing Activity:

Ask students to tell about places they have visited on trips. Make a list of these places and of places the class would like to visit. Say that it would be nice to be in the shoes of people who have gone to these places; instead, let's find out about these places and use our own shoeprints to tell others about them.

Writing Project:

Divide the class into small groups. Have them help each other trace the outline of both of their shoes onto construction paper. Cut the shoeprints out. Tell the groups to talk about places they would like to visit. Decide as a group where they would like to go. Each group's location must be in a different state or country. Have each group member answer one or more of the following questions and write the answer on their shoeprint.

1. How did you get there and how long did it take?
2. Where did you stay?
3. What did the place look like? (Give good details.)
4. What did you do there? (Shops, restaurants, tourist attractions, etc.) Several people could work on this.
5. How long did you stay and how did you get home?

Make a label with the place name on it and hang the shoeprints above or below it. Or, string the label and shoeprints together for a travel mobile.

TASTY TREAT

Materials:

- **Copies of ice cream treat patterns (pages 32-34)**
- **Crayons, Scissors**

Pre-writing Activity:

Show students pictures of different desserts--pies, cakes, cookies, ice cream etc. Brainstorm with the class about their favorite desserts. Make a list on the board. Take a poll to see what is the students' favorite treat. This could be done by graphing choices.

Writing Project:

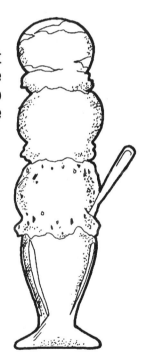

Divide the class into groups. Give each group a set of tasty treat patterns (pages 32-34). They will need multiple copies of the ice cream scoops on page 34. Tell them they are to work together to assemble a written treat for their group. There are several ways to use the treat patterns.

1. Story parts can be written on the banana and ice cream scoops and then assembled to make one big banana split of a story.

2. Students can use the pieces to analyze a story. One student could describe the setting on the top scoop of ice cream. Another could write about the characters on the next scoop and a third could state the story's problem. These could be assembled in the soda glass on which the solution or conclusion of the story has been written.

Patterns can be enlarged for even bigger treats and students can add their own toppings--cherries, nuts, syrup, whipped cream, etc. before displaying.

Possible Story Starters

The Day I Ate Too Many Chocolate Sundaes

Ingredients for Friendship

The Biggest Banana Split in the World

The Ice Cream Eating Contest

A Strawberry Sundae as Big as a Mountain

DISH AND BANANA FOR TASTY TREAT

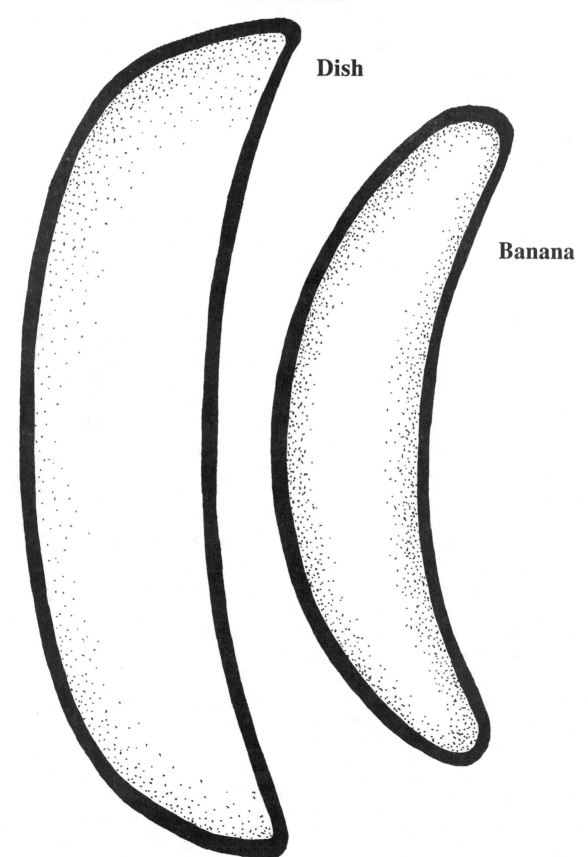

Dish

Banana

SODA GLASS FOR TASTY TREAT

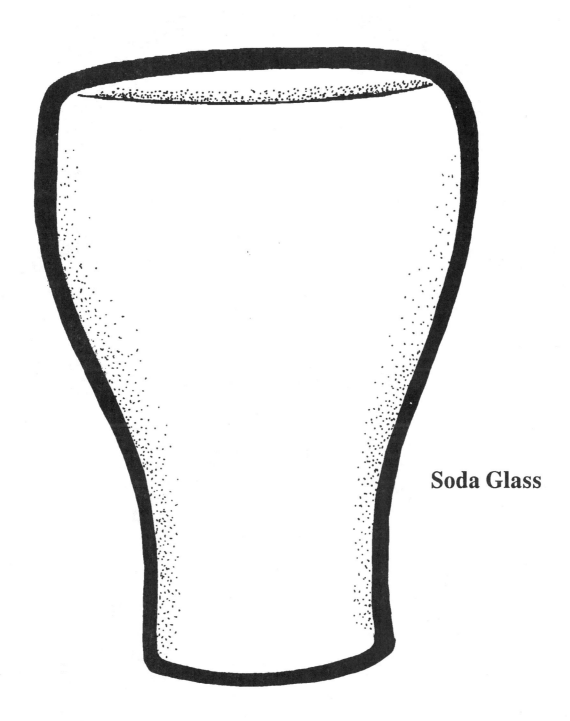

Soda Glass

ICE CREAM SCOOPS FOR TASTY TREAT

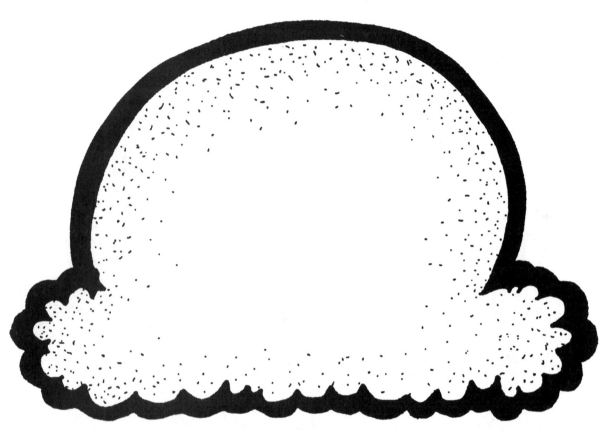

Ice Cream Scoops

FOLD - OUT CHARACTER BOOK

Materials:

- Heavy paper for cover, pages and back of book

- Writing and drawing paper same size or slightly smaller than book pages

- A fold-out character (pages 36-39) for each group

- Crayons, Scissors, Glue, Yarn or Rings for joining pages

Pre-writing Activity:

Tell or read the story of *The Emperor's New Clothes*. Point out that this story has a strong main character who really knows what he wants.

Writing Project:

Divide the class into groups. Each group should think of a story with one of the fold-out characters as its main character. The story should emphasize something that the character really wants or does not want. It can be clothing like the emperor or toys, cars, food, anything. Each group member should write one page of the story. When the writing is finished, the group should proofread and edit it before making a final copy. Each page should be illustrated on a separate sheet of paper.

Assembling the Book:

1. Write the title on one sheet of heavy paper and decorate. This will be the front of the cover.

2. Cut out the parts for the chosen character from page 36, 37, 38, or 39. Glue the tabs of the character parts to the **inside** of the book cover so that the character faces away from the book title--head and left arm on top, legs on bottom, and right arm on the outside edge. To hide the tabs, glue a sheet of paper to the inside of the cover.

3. Punch aligned holes through the heavy paper for the cover, blank pages, and back of book. Use yarn (loosely tied) or rings (available in office supply or stationery stores) to join the pages. The group's work should be copied onto or attached to the book pages with an illustration on the left hand page and the matching story on the right hand page. Fold the character parts inward when closing the book.

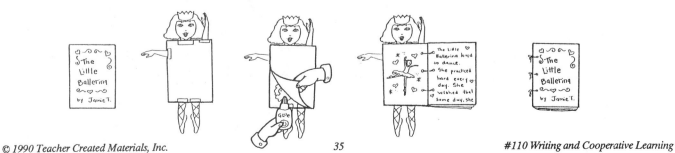

FOLD - OUT CHARACTER BOOK

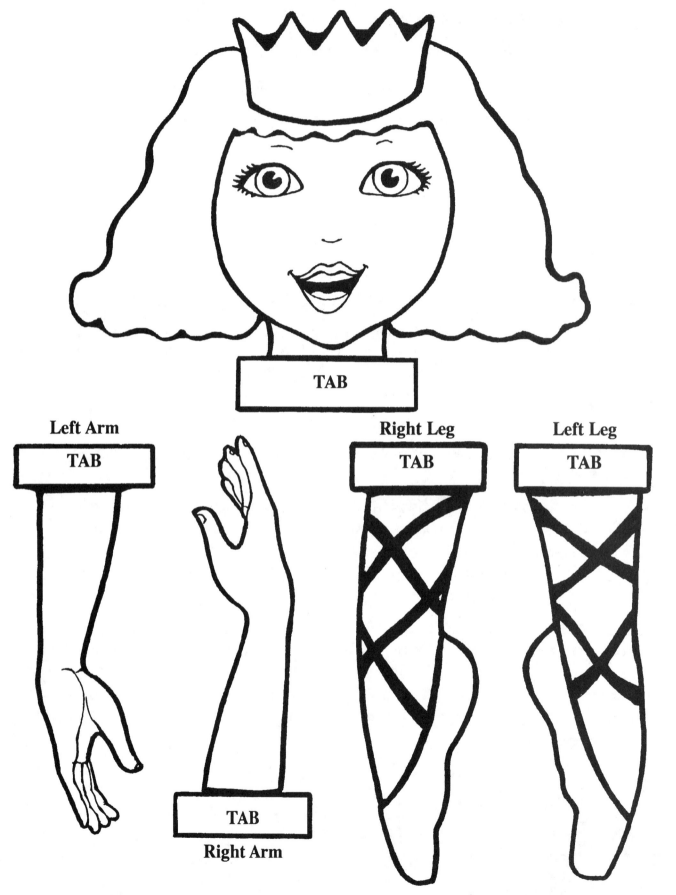

TAB

Left Arm

TAB

Right Leg

TAB

Left Leg

TAB

TAB

Right Arm

FOLD - OUT CHARACTER BOOK

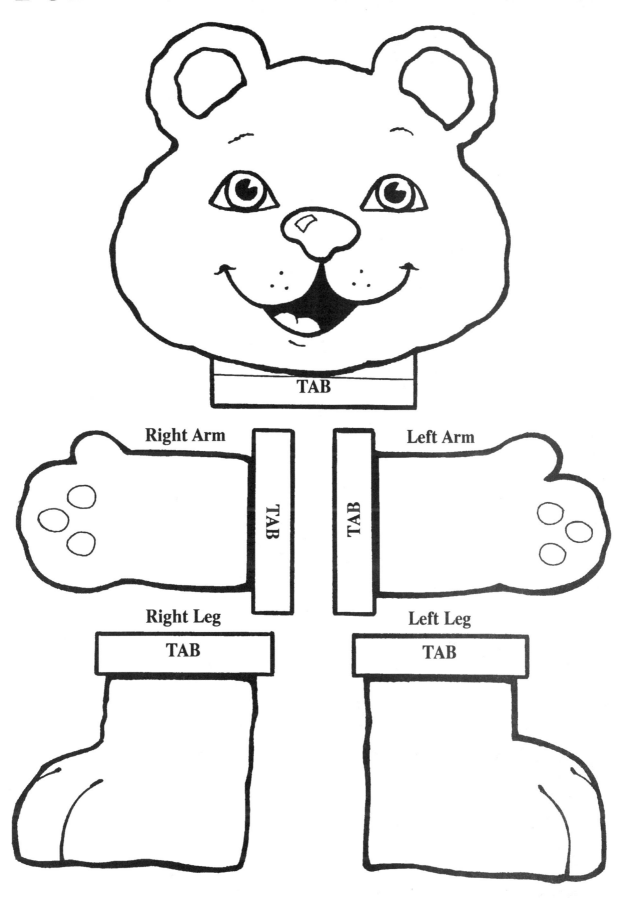

FOLD - OUT CHARACTER BOOK

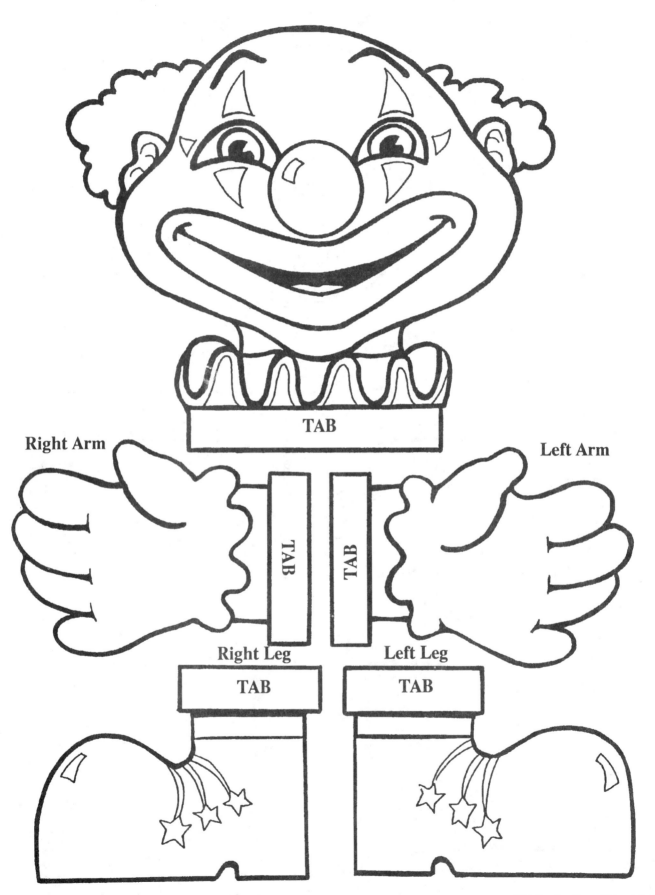

TAB

Right Arm

Left Arm

TAB

TAB

Right Leg

Left Leg

TAB

TAB

FOLD - OUT CHARACTER BOOK

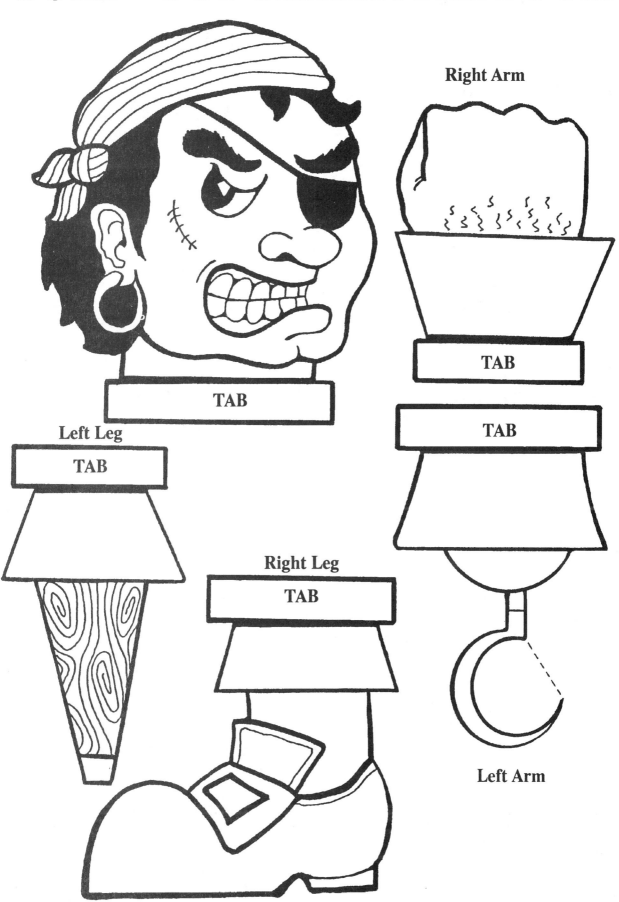

Right Arm

TAB

TAB

Left Leg

TAB

Right Leg

TAB

Left Arm

STORIES WITH COLOR

Materials:

- **Blank pages and cover materials for a Big Book**

- **Crayons or marking pens**

Pre-writing Activity:

Ask students how it would look if the world were without color. Tell the students that they are going to add a little color to the world with colorful stories.

Writing Project:

Divide the class into groups. Tell each child to choose one of the following story starters or make up their own and write a short story.

The Bright Orange House Down the Street

Black Bear and the Red Skates

The Day Everyone Turned Green

The Purple Plum that Fell from the Red Apple Tree

The Girl Who Turned Red into Yellow

The Adventures of the Red Rubber Boots

The Day Everyone's Sneakers Turned Purple

The Day All Colors Disappeared

The group should proofread each other's work, then the stories should be copied onto the pages for the Big Book and illustrated with nice, bright colors. Everyone should agree on a title which should be written on the cover and the pages should be put together to form a very color-full Big Book.

BOOK OF MEMORIES

Pre-writing Activity:

Materials:

• **Paper, Crayons**

Tell the students a story about one of your fondest memories. Include things that trigger the memory--smells, sounds, photographs, food. Let the children tell about a time that they would like to relive. This should trigger positive memories for them to report to the class. Probe to elicit details about the memory--the sights, sounds, and smells that accompanied it.

Writing Project:

Divide the students into groups. Each student should write about a special memory including many details and have it proofread by the group. The memory story should be copied onto paper for a memory book and signed at the bottom. It should be illustrated on a separate page. The final copies and illustrations should be be put into a Book of Memories to which students may add when another special occasion becomes a pleasant memory.

I remember...

I WONDER BOOKS

Materials:

- **I Wonder Cards from pages 43 and 44**
- **Paper, Crayons**

Pre-writing Activity:

Read "The Unicorn" by Shel Silverstein, **Where the Sidewalk Ends**, and/or a few of Rudyard Kipling's **Just So Stories** (e.g., "How the Camel Got His Hump," "How the Leopard Got His Spots," "The Elephant's Child") to the class. Help them identify the common element of these stories and poem--the fantasized explanation of nature.

Writing Project:

Duplicate and cut out cards on pages 43 and 44. Place them in a box. Divide the class into pairs and have each pair draw a card from the box. Together they should write a fantasy which answers the question on the card. They should find another pair to trade papers for proofreading and then make a neat copy. If you wish, you may allow students to glue their card to the top of their good copy for a title. The story should be illustrated and then bound into a class book of "I Wonder..." stories.

Extension: Have students add their own "I Wonder" cards to the box.

I WONDER CARDS

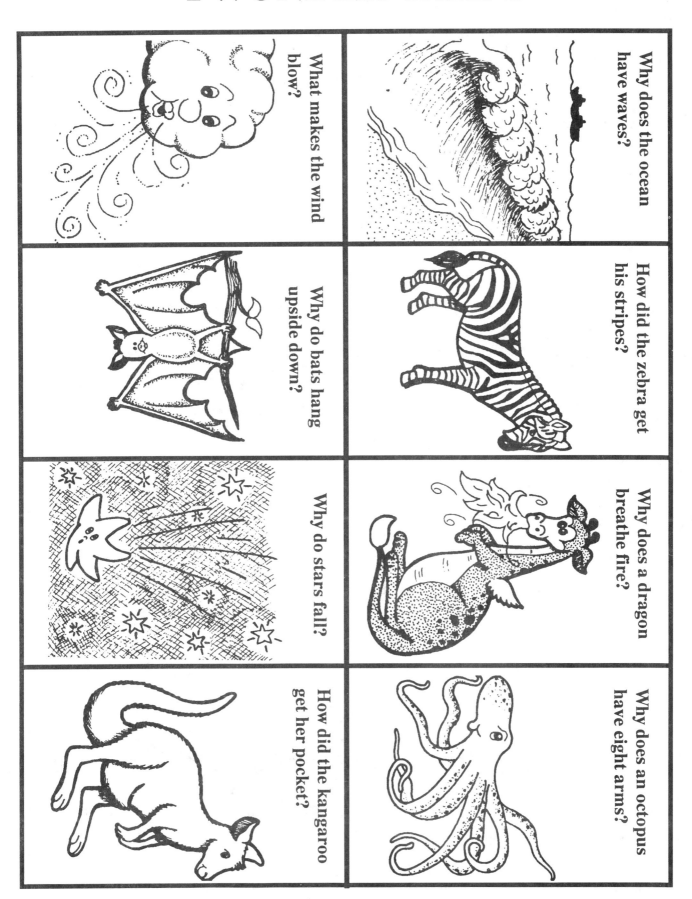

I WONDER CARDS

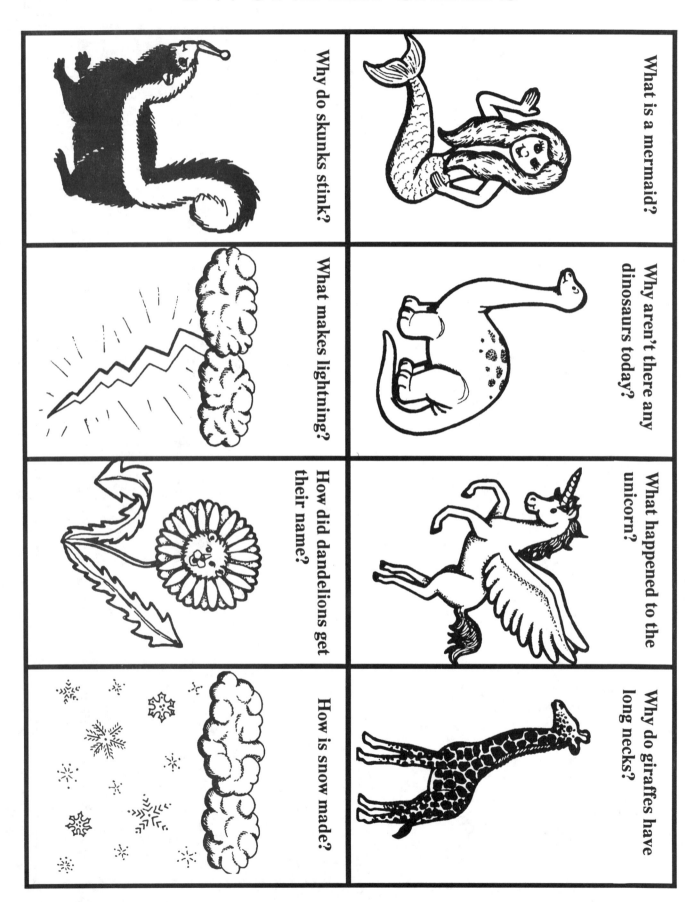

What is a mermaid?

Why do skunks stink?

Why aren't there any dinosaurs today?

What makes lightning?

What happened to the unicorn?

How did dandelions get their name?

Why do giraffes have long necks?

How is snow made?

ACCORDION CIRCUS BOOKS

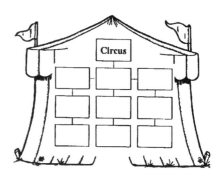

Materials:

- **Strips of paper 5 1/2" X 49 1/2" (butcher paper works well) for each group**

- **Two copies of the circus tent (page 46) for each group**

- **Crayons, Writing paper cut to 5" X 9" for each student**

Pre-writing Activity:

Brainstorm with the class about all the things associated with a circus. Record and classify their ideas using a diagram similar to the one above.

Writing Project:

Give each student a 5" X 9" piece of writing paper. Younger students may each write their own story about one of the circus items. Older students may work in groups of 5 to write a longer circus story. When the stories are finished, they should be shared for proofreading and neat copies should be made.

Assembling the Book:

1. Mark off one inch on each end of the long strips of paper. These will be the tabs for attaching the circus tent.

2. Fold the rest of the paper accordion fashion into five sections, each 9 1/2" long.

3. Attach a circus tent to each end of the strip and mount the circus stories on the folded sections.

4. Close the book and write the title and authors on the front page and THE END on the back tent.

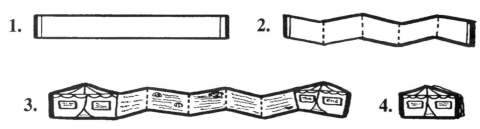

ACCORDION CIRCUS BOOK PATTERN

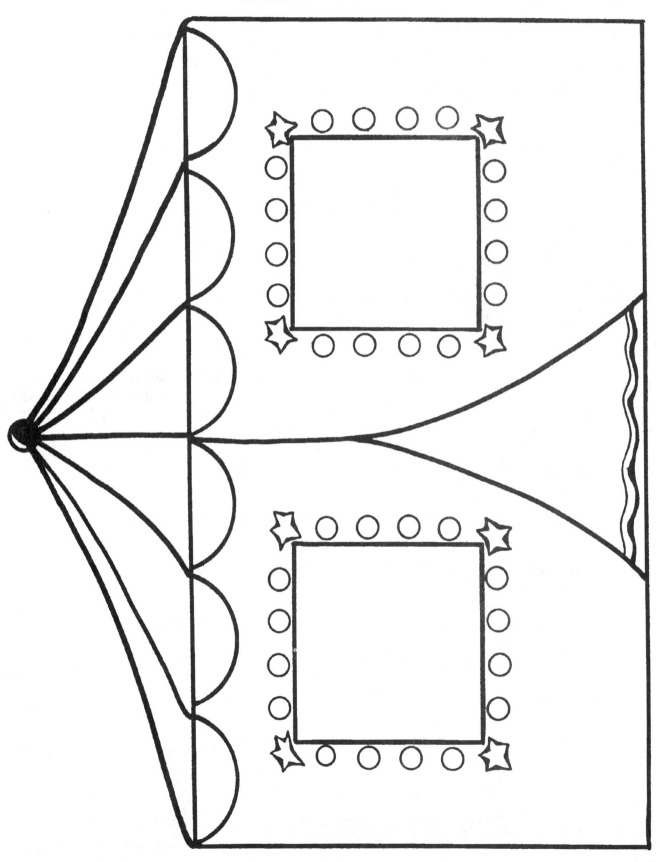

CALENDAR FOR THE FUTURE

Materials:

- **Copies of blank calendar (page 48)**
- **Crayons**

Pre-writing Activity:

Display and discuss the type of calendar that lists an important event on each date.

Writing Activity:

Divide students into small groups to make a calendar of the type discussed, but for the future. They will have to imagine events that will occur on the days of a month in a year of their choice. Group members may include themselves as if they have accomplished something of importance. Tell them to use their interests and imaginations to think of events that might happen and record them on each day of the calendar. Have them decorate the calendar being sure to include the month and year. They might even wish to research or calculate in order to get the dates on the correct days of the week for the year they have chosen. It will be fun to share these future calendars.

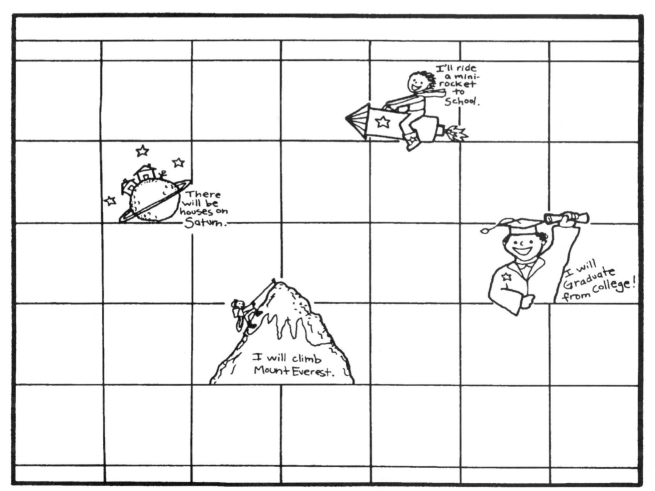

BLANK CALENDAR